NEW ORLEANS BUCKET LIST

Laissez les bon temps rouler!

L.M. ADKINS

D.L. SLOAN

PHANTOM PRESS
NEW ORLEANS | KEY WEST

Editorial services: DorothyDrennen.com

Inquiries: theneworleansbucketlist@gmail.com

Cover art © 2021 Shakor | gallerycayenne.com

HOW TO USE

1. **WHAT TO EXPECT:** This isn't a guidebook that holds your hand each step of the way. Instead, the book lists 100 offbeat adventures in New Orleans and provides a bit of local commentary to give you an idea of what's in store. Consider each page a primer for adventure. They are in no particular order.

2. **FINDING THINGS:** We've provided a custom google map at *phantompress.com/maps.* URLs and addresses are included with each adventure. Use your smartphone for accurate directions. Ask a local for interesting directions. Things change rapidly in New Orleans, so don't take it personally if an adventure has changed, moved, or gone away. Enjoy the journey. We added ten bonus adventures to make up for any that may change or close before the next edition is released.

3. **WARNINGS:** Some activities may be dangerous or illegal. Use common sense. Do them all at your own risk.

4. **BEST RESULTS:** Go at your own pace. If one of the items looks stupid to you — skip it. If you are unsure about an item — Google it. If you love an item — check it off twice. Bucket lists are about personal growth and achievement. Stepping out of your comfort zone is good. No matter how you approach the offbeat adventures in this book, you'll find that the best things about doing them are the memories you create and the people you meet along the way.

5. **SHARE:** Share your adventures with the hashtags on each page and #nolabucket

A NOTE FROM THE AUTHORS

Thanks for buying The New Orleans Bucket List.

Our goal is to deliver offbeat adventures to you in an honest and entertaining fashion that will make it easy for you to plan your New Orleans experiences without wasting your time.

Nobody paid to be in this book. The people and places recommended are included because they have solid reputations. Most don't even know they are included, but feel free to tell them!

Things are changing rapidly this year. If an adventure has moved, closed, or significantly changed from how it is described, please send us a note, and we will update that adventure in the next edition.

Thanks for kicking it in New Orleans.

Loretta-Maria Adkins   David L. Sloan

theneworleansbucketlist@gmail.com

ADVENTURES 1-25

1. DRINK A 360 AT THE CAROUSEL BAR
2. SEEK GUIDANCE FROM THE VOODOO QUEEN
3. YELL-A FOR STELLA
4. GO GA-GA FOR GUMBO
5. JAZZ IT UP AT PRESERVATION HALL
6. SNAP A SHOT WITH A BOURBON STREET SIGN
7. GASLIGHT YOURSELF
8. TAKE YOUR MEDS AT AMERICA'S FIRST PHARMACY
9. CIRCLE JACKSON SQUARE
10. PARTY UNDER "DA BRIDGE"
11. RIDE ON A FLOAT
12. HOP ON THE SAINT CHARLES STREETCAR
13. STROLL THE SCULPTURE GARDEN
14. FERRY TO THE WESTBANK
15. FIND THE PLASTIC BABY
16. GET LOCAL WITH A TOP CHEF
17. ATTEND MASS AT ST. LOUIS CATHEDRAL
18. WATCH BEIGNETS BEING MADE
19. SAY CHEESE AT WASHINGTON ARTILLERY PARK
20. FIND A SPANISH FLAG
21. MAKE A WISH IN THE SECOND LINE FOUNTAIN
22. LISTEN TO THE MAGICAL SINGING OAK
23. MISSISSIPPI MORNING MEDITATION
24. TAILGATE AT CHAMPIONS SQUARE
25. PARTY LIKE A CAJUN AT A FAIS DO-DO

ADVENTURES 25-50

ADVENTURES 51-75

ADVENTURES 76-100

BONUS ADVENTURES 101-110

Lagniappe is a Cajun French word describing a little something extra. A baker's dozen. A slice of pie at a restaurant after you have paid your check. 110 New Orleans Bucket List items when you were only promised 100.

101.	**TRAVERSE TULANE**
102.	**GET THRIFTY-STYLEY**
103.	**EAT A VIETNAMESE PO-BOY**
104.	**DOWNWARD DOG ON THE RIVERBANK**
105.	**TRY ON BIG HATS**
106.	**JAZZ IT UP**
107.	**STROLL LONGUE VUE GARDENS**
108.	**GET WIGGY WITH IT**
109.	**STALK THE RICH AND FAMOUS**
110.	**SAY FAREWELL WITH A TOAST**

1

DRINK A 360 AT THE CAROUSEL BAR

WHAT'S THE DEAL? Hotel Monteleone *(214 Royal Street, hotelmonteleone.com)* has one of the world's most iconic bars. The Carousel Bar & Lounge is designed like an old-time carousel, complete with revolving bar stools. You can't leave New Orleans without sipping through a full rotation.

DO IT IF: You like horsing around.

SKIP IT IF: You don't need a rotating bar to get the spins.

LOCAL ADVICE: Order a Vieux Carré. The drink is named after the French Quarter and was first created in the Hotel Monteleone in the 1930s.

I DID IT: ☐ #nolabucket #nolaspins

DID YOU KNOW?

Hotel Monteleone's celebrity guests include Liberace, Ernest Hemingway, Tennessee Williams, William Faulkner, Truman Capote, Michael Jordan, and Dennis Quaid.

2

SEEK GUIDANCE FROM THE VOODOO QUEEN

WHAT'S THE DEAL? Marie Laveau is the Voodoo Queen of New Orleans. She died in 1881, but genuine practitioners of this African-based religion call forth the spirits and petition her on your behalf. Voodoo Authentica *(612 Dumaine St., voodooshop.com)* was established in 1996. This is an excellent spot for readings and an authentic taste of New Orleans Voodoo.

DO IT IF: You're yearning to sit for a spell.

SKIP IT IF: You "don't mess around with that Voodoo sh*t."

LOCAL ADVICE: Research your reader before committing to a ceremony. Marie Laveau's tomb is in the St. Louis #1 Cemetery if you want to go right to the source. The cemetery can only be visited with a licensed tour guide. (cemeterytoursneworleans.com) Pay a visit to Nicholas Cage's pyramid-shaped tomb while you are at it.

I DID IT: ☐   #nolabucket #voodoosh*t

DID YOU KNOW?

One of the reasons Marie Laveau was so popular in New Orleans in the 1800s was because she syncretized Catholicism and the Vo-dun religion of Africa.

3

YELL-A FOR STELLA

WHAT'S THE DEAL? Tennessee Williams lived in New Orleans for more than 40 years and wrote some of his best works about the colorful characters he encountered here. Locals pay tribute to the literary great each March with a Tennessee Williams Festival. A highlight is the Stanley/Stella Shouting Contest. It recreates the famous scene from A Streetcar Named Desire under the Pontalba Apartments' balcony *(501 St. Ann Street, corner of Decatur Street)*. Don't sweat it if you are not here in March. Belt out your best "Stella" any time of year. If anybody looks at you strangely, tell them Tennessee sent you.

DO IT IF: You feel tragic like you're Marlon Brando.

SKIP IT IF: You are with your new wife, and your last wife was named Stella.

LOCAL ADVICE: Tennessee Williams lived in an apartment at 632 1/2 St. Peter Street while writing A Streetcar Named Desire. Visit the Historic New Orleans Collection *(520 Royal St., hnok.org)* to learn about his other residences.

I DID IT: ☐ #nolabucket #yellafever

DID YOU KNOW?

A Streetcar Named Desire was originally called A Poker Night. Williams changed its title and named it after the streetcar line running through the French Quarter to Desire Street.

4

GO GA-GA FOR GUMBO

WHAT'S THE DEAL? Gumbo is a stew that may contain ingredients ranging from shrimp and okra to sausage or rabbit. The true spirit of gumbo is to make your best batch with whatever life blessed or cursed you with. This makes every bowl a treat and a surprise and puts gumbo at the top of the list of foods you must try in New Orleans.

DO IT IF: You will play for gumbo.

SKIP IT IF: You have a history with shellfish and anaphylactic shock.

LOCAL ADVICE: Do it the Cajun way and order a side of potato salad with your gumbo. Get a spoonful of potato salad and dip it into the gumbo on the way to your mouth. Mais yeah!

I DID IT: ☐ #nolabucket #gagagumbo

DID YOU KNOW?

The name gumbo comes from a West African word for okra. "File," as in "file gumbo" is ground up sassafras leaves and was likely first added by Native Americans.

5

JAZZ IT UP AT PRESERVATION HALL

WHAT'S THE DEAL? This little hole in the wall *(726 St. Peter St., preservationhall.com)* has been honoring New Orleans Jazz music traditions and the musicians who carry the torch since 1961. The performances are magical and memorable. There are several shows a night over 350 nights a year.

DO IT IF: You have pizzazz for jazz.

SKIP IT IF: Your spouse left you for a jazz musician.

LOCAL ADVICE: Buy your tickets in advance online to avoid the lines of people waiting for cheap seats.

I DID IT: ☐ #nolabucket #jazzhands

DID YOU KNOW?

The Preservation Hall Jazz Band has traveled the world, playing with everyone from The Grateful Dead to the King of Thailand (who sat in on alto sax.)

6

SNAP A SHOT WITH A BOURBON STREET SIGN

WHAT'S THE DEAL? Nearly everyone has seen the image of the red-nosed, disheveled hobo hanging on the Bourbon Street lamppost. His social media accounts were suspended, so it is up to you to carry the torch. Find a corner, strike a pose, and share it with the world so they have no doubt about where you are.

DO IT IF: You like getting boozed up and recreating iconic images.

SKIP IT IF: You don't want your boss to know why you called in sick this week.

LOCAL ADVICE: Go to lower Bourbon Street. It's more residential, and you won't have to wait your turn behind fellow drunks.

I DID IT: ☐ #nolabucket #bourbonshot

DID YOU KNOW?

Bourbon Street was named after the ruling French Dynasty when Louisiana was settled. Bourbon County, KY, was part of the Louisiana Territory. This is the county where bourbon is distilled. Coincidence? I think not...

7

GASLIGHT YOURSELF

WHAT'S THE DEAL? Charming gaslights are still widely used outside homes on the cobblestone streets in the French Quarter. Most of them are made in New Orleans by a company called Bevolo *(521 Conti St., bevolo.com)*. You can watch these magical lights being constructed in the old tradition by master craftsmen in a workshop behind their showroom.

DO IT IF: You have a gas exploring aspects of New Orleans architecture.

SKIP IT IF: You have gas.

LOCAL ADVICE: Visit before 3 pm if you want to watch the craftsmen at work.

I DID IT: ☐ #nolabucket #gaslighting

DID YOU KNOW?

The Bevolo brand of the copper lantern is in all 50 states and over 50 countries. Today, the lanterns use mostly natural gas, a change from the animal fat they used in Europe when the lanterns first became popular.

TAKE YOUR MEDS AT AMERICA'S FIRST PHARMACY

WHAT'S THE DEAL? Louis Joseph Dufilho, Jr. opened America's first licensed pharmacy in New Orleans in 1823. Today, it operates as The New Orleans Pharmacy Museum *(514 Chartres St., pharmacymuseum.org)*. The walls are lined with the pharmacy's history, ranging from intriguing to bizarre. Bring a daily pill of your own and pop it discreetly once inside.

DO IT IF: You want to step into a pharmaceutical time machine.

SKIP IT IF: Your daily pill is Viagra.

LOCAL ADVICE: Take a guided tour and ask about Love Potion Number Nine. Don't miss the obstetrics exhibit.

I DID IT: ☐ #nolabucket #pharmasee

DID YOU KNOW?

The first pharmaceutical licensing test was administered to Mr. Dufilho in the Cabildo by the first American Governor, William Claiborne. Before the advent of licensing, all you had to do to become a pharmacist was apprentice under another pharmacist for six months.

9

CIRCLE
JACKSON SQUARE

WHAT'S THE DEAL? Jackson Square *(701 Decatur St., nola.gov/parks-and-parkways/parks-squares/jackson-square)* is the heart of the French Quarter, and the French Quarter is the heart of New Orleans. Jugglers, tarot readers, painters, and musicians perform here daily. Circle the square for a real taste of the heartbeat of New Orleans. Find a spot to sit for an hour, and it will fill your cup with an array of humanity not found anywhere else in the world.

DO IT IF: You dig colorful characters.

SKIP IT IF: You can't handle anything named Jackson since Michael died.

LOCAL ADVICE: The statues in the corners of the square represent the four seasons. Visit each and see if you can guess which season it portrays.

I DID IT: ☐ #nolabucket #jacksonaction

DID YOU KNOW?

Jackson Square was initially an empty lot called "Place des Armes" and was used for military exercises and public executions.

10

PARTY UNDER "DA BRIDGE"

WHAT'S THE DEAL? Locals gather beneath Treme's Claiborne Avenue bridge every Sunday to let loose. Vendors sell smoked meats, homemade drinks, and other local delicacies. The music is loud, and the crowd knows how to party!

DO IT IF: You want to party with the locals.

SKIP IT IF: You hate crowds, loud music, and motorcycles.

LOCAL ADVICE: Hang out by Kermit's Treme Mother-in-Law Lounge *(1500 N. Claiborne Ave.)* for great drinks to go and live music.

I DID IT: ☐ #nolabucket #bridgetroll

DID YOU KNOW?

New Orleans' longest street is named after the first governor of Louisiana, William C.C. Claiborne.

11

RIDE ON A FLOAT

WHAT'S THE DEAL? Mardi Gras has the most celebrated parades and floats, but New Orleans has parades all year. Many organizations called "krewes" accept new members or even one-time parade participants for a fee. Get ready for the ride of your life.

DO IT IF: You want to know how a rock star feels on stage.

SKIP IT IF: You prefer to be a groupie.

LOCAL ADVICE: Find a parade organization outside of the city. They usually have more reasonable buy-in rates for a one-timer. Outside of Mardi Gras, holidays like Saint Patrick's Day also have some lenient requirements for new riders. Check Craigslist or local classifieds for people selling their spot.

I DID IT: ☐ #nolabucket #ifloated

DID YOU KNOW?

Mardi Gras was first celebrated in New Orleans in 1699. The first parade rolled in 1709. The first krewe, formed in 1856, is the "Mystick Krewe of Comus."

12

HOP ON THE SAINT CHARLES STREETCAR

WHAT'S THE DEAL? The Saint Charles Streetcar Line *(norta.com)* is one of America's most scenic public transportation rides. Live oaks, antebellum mansions, college campuses, and Audubon Park are highlights.

DO IT IF: You love unusual types of public transportation.

SKIP IT IF: Your butt can't handle wooden seats and a little heat in the summer.

LOCAL ADVICE: Get off at the Riverbend and eat lunch at the Camellia Grill. You can pay on the streetcar or buy day passes at any Walgreens or on the RTA app. Sit on one side going up, and the other on the way back.

I DID IT: ☐   #nolabucket #streetcar

DID YOU KNOW?

On this line, the dark green cars are registered with the National Register of Historic Places and have remained unaltered for 150 years.

13

STROLL THE SCULPTURE GARDEN

WHAT'S THE DEAL? New Orleans Museum of Art *(1 Collins Diboll Cir., noma.org)* is famous the world over for its collection of modern art. The Sydney and Walda Besthoff Sculpture Garden boasts more than 90 sculptures across 11 acres of mature native trees surrounding two lagoons.

DO IT IF: You like art, nature, and strolling.

SKIP IT IF: You prefer your art served in a frosted mug on Bourbon Street.

LOCAL ADVICE: Check the NOLA Project *(nolaproject.com)* for notable productions in the garden. Try to catch a giant puppet show.

I DID IT: ☐   #nolabucket #besthoffbothworlds

DID YOU KNOW?

Louisiana Irises are some of the most popular native plants showcased in the garden. They replaced the European Irises which were wiped out during Hurricane Katrina.

14

FERRY TO THE WESTBANK

WHAT'S THE DEAL? The New Orleans skyline's best views happen on a Canal Street Ferry *(1 Canal St., norta.com)* crossing to the Westbank. The 30-minute trip takes you across the Mississippi River to the historic neighborhood of Algiers Point. Here you can stroll the Jazz Walk of Fame or grab a bite in a local café.

DO IT IF: You've never crossed the Mississippi River.

SKIP IT IF: You get seasick and have a fear of ferries.

LOCAL ADVICE: Rent a bike and bring it along so you can explore the levees and streets of old Algiers. Grab a drink at the Old Point Bar *(545 Patterson Rd., oldpointbarnola.com).*

I DID IT: ☐ #nolabucket #bankshot

DID YOU KNOW?

Built-up along the riverfront in 1819, Algiers is New Orleans' second oldest neighborhood. Many films and television shows are shot here.

15

FIND THE PLASTIC BABY

WHAT'S THE DEAL? King Cake is a New Orleans Mardi Gras delicacy descended from a traditional French cake called "Galette des Rois." Hidden inside each cake is a plastic baby. Finding the baby in your slice is good luck and earns you the title of "king" or "queen" for the day, but beware: you will also be responsible for buying the next King Cake or throwing the next King Cake party.

DO IT IF: You like cake and want a story about the time you almost ate a baby in New Orleans.

SKIP IT IF: You are frugal and have a fear of choking on small plastic objects.

LOCAL ADVICE: The King Cake Hub *(1464 S. Broad St. at Zony Mash and 520 Royal St. at the Historic New Orleans Connection, kingcakehub.com)* has King Cakes from all of New Orleans' best bakeries in one convenient spot.

I DID IT: ☐   #nolabucket #ieatbabies

DID YOU KNOW?

It is considered bad luck to eat King Cake outside of Carnival season. Superstitions range from "It will rain on Mardi Gras Day" to "The Saints will lose the Super Bowl." As a tourist, you can find it year-round but you should consider the possible consequences!

16

GET LOCAL WITH A TOP CHEF

WHAT'S THE DEAL? Crescent City Farmers Market *(crescentcityfarmersmarket.org)* is a producer-only farmers market connecting customers directly with farmers, fishermen, ranchers, dairy farmers, bakers, and food makers from within 200 miles of the Crescent City. Our top chefs present cooking demonstrations at the market showcasing local products and unique recipes. See their website at *crescentcityfarmersmarket.org* for up-to-date locations.

DO IT IF: You like to stalk culinary experts.

SKIP IT IF: The only thing you make for dinner is reservations.

LOCAL ADVICE: Look for the popsicles on a hot day, and try the avocado one!

I DID IT: ☐ #nolabucket #farmished

DID YOU KNOW?

The Crescent City Farmers Market has three locations, attracting 132,396 visitors each year.

17

ATTEND MASS AT ST. LOUIS CATHEDRAL

WHAT'S THE DEAL? Saint Louis Cathedral *(615 Pere Antoine Alley, stlouiscathedral.org)* is the oldest Catholic cathedral in continual use in the United States. Regardless of your religious orientation, attending a mass in this beautiful Basilica is an experience that will leave you feeling uplifted and joyful.

DO IT IF: You love organ music and historically significant places of worship.

SKIP IT IF: You feel a burning sensation every time you step foot in a church.

LOCAL ADVICE: The most popular mass of the week is on Sunday morning at 11.

I DID IT: ☐ #nolabucket #burningforyou

DID YOU KNOW?

Friar Antonio de Sedella, known by his parishioners as Père Antoine, is said to haunt the cathedral. He is buried there, and people report his apparition roaming the alley that bears his name alongside the church.

18

WATCH BEIGNETS BEING MADE

WHAT'S THE DEAL? Café du Monde *(800 Decatur St., cafedumonde.com)* is the oldest coffee stand in New Orleans. Devouring an order of beignets and a café au lait here is a rite of passage. Most people overlook the window in the alley behind the café. Here, you can see staff making beignets 24 hours a day, 7 days a week, 364 days a year.

DO IT IF: You love looking at food, even when you are not eating it.

SKIP IT IF: Powdered sugar triggers your cocaine addiction.

LOCAL ADVICE: Go before 10 am to avoid a crowd at the window. Bring cash if you plan to eat. Café du Monde does not take credit cards.

I DID IT: ☐ #nolabucket #scarfface

DID YOU KNOW?

Café du Monde has operated in New Orleans since 1862 and is as famous for their coffee with chicory as their beignets. Chicory was an herb that Europeans added to their coffee to stretch their supply when it was running low. People came to appreciate the taste, and now it is a New Orleans staple.

19

SAY CHEESE AT WASHINGTON ARTILLERY PARK

WHAT'S THE DEAL? Washington Artillery Park *(768 Decatur St., washingtonartillery.com)* provides one of the most scenic overlooks in the city. The iconic views of Jackson Square and Saint Louis Cathedral are Instagram favorites. Whether you ask a stranger for help or take a selfie, this is a photo opportunity you don't want to miss.

DO IT IF: You want to pose like an influencer.

SKIP IT IF: You are in the witness protection program.

LOCAL ADVICE: Visit the park at sunset for one of the most beautiful cityscape pictures you will take in the Big Easy.

I DID IT: ☐ #nolabucket #heavyartillery

DID YOU KNOW?

The Washington Artillery is one of Louisiana's oldest militia units. It was initially known as *Compagnie de Milice de la Louisiane* (Militia Company of Louisiana). It was renamed for George Washington in the late 1700s.

20

FIND A SPANISH FLAG

WHAT'S THE DEAL? While the city of New Orleans was established as a colony by France, it was passed to Spain in 1762. It remained a Spanish colony until shortly before the Louisiana purchase. There are a handful of Spanish flags scattered throughout the French Quarter. Searching for one adds an extra element of excitement to your travels and leads to countless unique discoveries you might otherwise miss.

DO IT IF: You like scavenger hunts.

SKIP IT IF: The rain in Spain falls mainly on your brain.

LOCAL ADVICE: Hint* Look to places of lodging. You may also find an abundance of Spanish tile – look at the street name tiles and the ones around the fountain at Spanish Plaza.

I DID IT: ☐ #nolabucket #spanishrule

DID YOU KNOW?

New Orleans was unceremoniously passed from France to Spain in 1873 as part of a back-room deal called "The Treaty of Paris," designed to keep the city from falling into the hands of the British. New Orleans remained a Spanish colony until 1802 when Napoleon reclaimed it and sold it to the United States in the Louisiana Purchase.

21

MAKE A WISH IN THE SECOND LINE FOUNTAIN

WHAT'S THE DEAL? The Second Line is a New Orleans parade tradition. A colorful fountain at the foot of Dumaine Street *(400 Dumaine St.)* honors these processions. It makes a perfect spot to have a seat and rest your feet while throwing a coin in the fountain.

DO IT IF: You have spare change and lots of wishes.

SKIP IT IF: You are concerned about reports of a coin shortage.

LOCAL ADVICE: The fountain is a short walk from Café du Monde and a great spot to eat beignets.

I DID IT: ☐ #nolabucket #dropaline

DID YOU KNOW?

Second Lines are descendants of New Orleans funeral processions, but you can find them celebrating weddings, bachelor parties, and birthdays. You don't need an invitation to be part of a Second Line—just jump in and join the fun.

22

LISTEN TO THE MAGICAL SINGING OAK

WHAT'S THE DEAL? City Park *(1701 Wisner Blvd., neworleanscitypark.com)* is home to an ancient, magnificent, live oak tree with several giant wind chimes suspended from her branches. There is a bench to support you as you soak up the sounds and relax.

DO IT IF: You need to decompress before you kill somebody.

SKIP IT IF: The sound of wind chimes makes you want to kill somebody.

LOCAL ADVICE: The oak is to the right of the main entrance next to Big Lake. Go on a windy day; the breezier, the better!

I DID IT: ☐ #nolabucket #magicoak

DID YOU KNOW?

The chimes were hung by local artist Jim Hart and are tuned to ring out in the pentatonic scale. They are painted black to blend in with the plant's natural shadows. One of them is 14 feet long.

23

MISSISSIPPI MORNING MEDITATION

WHAT'S THE DEAL? The mighty Mississippi River is the lifeblood of the city of New Orleans. Starting your day on her banks watching the water flow is a unique spiritual adventure that can help you get grounded before a day of exploring.

DO IT IF: Big wheel, keep on turning.

SKIP IT IF: Pumped a lot of pain down in New Orleans.

LOCAL ADVICE: Go early in the morning, but wait until the sun is up and the unsavory characters of the night have gone home.

I DID IT: ☐ #nolabucket #mississippimorn

DID YOU KNOW?

New Orleans is called "The Crescent City" after the shape of a bend in the Mississippi River close to the French Quarter.

24

TAILGATE AT CHAMPIONS SQUARE

WHAT'S THE DEAL? The New Orleans Saints football team is the pride of New Orleans, and tailgating for a game is a favorite local pastime. If you can't get tickets to a home game, you can party like a rock star at Champions Square *(Lasalle St., champions-square.com)* with big screen tv action and some of the best food and drink vendors in the city.

DO IT IF: You love football and tailgating.

SKIP IT IF: You're a fan of the Falcons. Or the Rams. Or the Vikings.

LOCAL ADVICE: Wear black and gold if you want to fit in. "Who Dat!" is our battle cry.

I DID IT: ☐   #nolabucket #wearethechampions

DID YOU KNOW?

Superstitious residents blame any New Orleans Saints' losses on the Superdome's proximity to the former Girod Street cemetery, which is said to be right underneath the stadium.

25

PARTY LIKE A CAJUN AT A FAIS DO-DO

WHAT'S THE DEAL? The Fais do-do is a Cajun dance party, often held out in the country, defined by eating, drinking, dancing, and Zydeco music.

DO IT IF: You want to learn the Cajun two-step.

SKIP IT IF: You have two left feet and hate accordions.

LOCAL ADVICE: If you don't wrangle an invite to the real deal, Mulate's New Orleans Cajun Restaurant *(201 Julia St., mulates.com)* has live Cajun music nightly.

I DID IT: ☐ #nolabucket #faisdodo

DID YOU KNOW?

"Fais do-do" is a phrase young mothers said to their infants when they wanted the children to go to sleep so they could return to the dance floor.

26

TOUR THE SITE OF THE BATTLE OF NEW ORLEANS

WHAT'S THE DEAL? The Chalmette Battlefield *(1 Battlefield Rd., nps.gov/jela/chalmette-battlefield.htm)* is the site of the infamous battle during the War of 1812 that kept New Orleans from becoming a British colony and propelled Andrew Jackson into the Presidency. The battlefield contains an 1830s house, rampart, monument, and exhibits for self-guided tours.

DO IT IF: You like walking around where people died.

SKIP IT IF: Traversing marshy fields with knees like yours is a battle.

LOCAL ADVICE: Go at 10:45 am or 2:45 pm to catch an informative talk about the battle.

I DID IT: ☐ #nolabucket #battleofnola

DID YOU KNOW?

The largest multi-cultural, multi-lingual civilian militia ever assembled in the United States fought in the Battle of New Orleans. The participants included enslaved Africans, Native Americans, free men of color, sharpshooters from Kentucky and Tennessee, and women.

27

WATCH A MARDI GRAS FLOAT BEING CONSTRUCTED

WHAT'S THE DEAL? Mardi Gras World *(1380 Port of New Orleans Pl., mardigrasworld.com)* is a magical studio space where artists design and build over 500 Carnival floats a year. They have opened their doors to visitors so you can see how the Mardi Gras magic is brought to life.

DO IT IF: Behind-the-scenes looks float your boat.

SKIP IT IF: The only float you're interested in is an inner tube in a swimming pool.

LOCAL ADVICE: Mardi Gras World offers a free shuttle from anywhere in the French Quarter.

I DID IT: ☐   #nolabucket #imfloating

DID YOU KNOW?

Mardi Gras World is in Kern Studios, established in 1932 when the first parade floats were garbage wagons pulled by mules.

28

RIDE A SWAN

WHAT'S THE DEAL? Swan paddle boats are an iconic piece of American history, becoming a fixture in urban parks as early as 1877. Head to Big Lake at City Park *(Big Lake, right off Friedrich's Ave.)* to rent one of these beauties *(wheelfunrentals.com)* and take in the local flora and fauna.

DO IT IF: You want to add "swan operator" to your resume.

SKIP IT IF: You think paddle boats are for the birds.

LOCAL ADVICE: For a little romance, rent one at night.

I DID IT: ☐ #nolabucket #swanlake

DID YOU KNOW?

This oasis in the city is home to creatures great and small, including turtles, fish, frogs, and hundreds of bird species.

29

DRINK IN A BORDELLO

WHAT'S THE DEAL? New Orleans' checkered past includes a district where prostitution was legalized for almost 20 years. May Baily's Place *(415 Dauphine St., dauphineorleans.com/may-bailys-place)* was a working brothel. Today, the Victorian-inspired lounge has been renovated to capture the spirit of that time, including pictures on the wall by noted Storyville photographer E.J. Bellocq.

DO IT IF: You are feeling saucy.

SKIP IT IF: A prostitute ruined your last marriage.

LOCAL ADVICE: Try a "Miss Kitty" cocktail and buy a pair of stockings.

I DID IT: ☐ #nolabucket #bordelloshots

DID YOU KNOW?

When prostitution was illegal, May Baily paid a year's worth of fines in advance, thus earning a "license" to operate an unlawful brothel! A copy of this license is hanging above the piano.

30

PAY HOMAGE TO LOUIS ARMSTRONG

WHAT'S THE DEAL? Louis Armstrong was a New Orleans trumpeter, vocalist, and composer, noted as one of the most influential figures in the history of jazz. Congo Square is an open space in Louis Armstrong Park *(701 N. Rampart St.)* that is celebrated as the birthplace of jazz music. Pay homage to Mr. Armstrong by putting on your headphones and blaring 'Satchmo' in the park that bears his name.

DO IT IF: You've seen trees of green, red roses too...

SKIP IT IF: You would rather stay home and toot your own horn.

LOCAL ADVICE: Bring a picnic lunch and reflect on your amazing life. Don't miss the rose garden.

I DID IT: ☐   #nolabucket #louisnotlance

DID YOU KNOW?

According to guidelines in the "Code Noir" established by the French, enslaved Africans were given Sundays off from their work. Congo Square was a place they could come to drum, dance, and speak in their native languages.

31

EXPERIENCE OAK STREET

WHAT'S THE DEAL? Uptown New Orleans has a super cool vibe, hip with college students, artists, and creatives. Dinner at Jacques-imo's *(8324 Oak St., jacques-imos.com)* and live music at the Maple Leaf Tavern (8316 Oak St) make a night that even the most loyal downtown denizens will cross Canal Street for.

DO IT IF: You've lost your taste for bourbon.

SKIP IT IF: You hate to wait. These hotspots can draw a crowd.

LOCAL ADVICE: Get a slice of alligator cheesecake at J-imo's. Tuesday night is Rebirth Brass Band Night at the Maple Leaf - that's the local fav. Take the St. Charles Avenue Street Car up.

I DID IT: ☐ #nolabucket #oakiedokie

DID YOU KNOW?

Oak Street's frequent appearance in movies helped New Orleans earn the nickname "Hollywood South."

32

EXPLORE A FORMER PLANTATION

WHAT'S THE DEAL? There are numerous antebellum plantation houses in and around New Orleans, throwbacks to the days when cotton was king and more millionaires lived in New Orleans than any other American city. Many are open for guided tours. Evergreen Plantation *(4677 LA-18, Edgard, evergreenplantation.org)* is a popular film location.

DO IT IF: You want to be gone with the wind.

SKIP IT IF: You can't handle learning about the suffering enslaved people endured.

LOCAL ADVICE: The Whitney Plantation Museum *(5099 LA-18, Edgard, whitneyplantation.org)* is the only museum in Louisiana that focuses exclusively on the lives of enslaved people. Make a reservation in advance.

I DID IT: ☐   #nolabucket #gonewiththewind

DID YOU KNOW?

Louisiana plantations grew sugar. Planters called their product "white gold" and generated fortunes on the backs of enslaved people. Before the Civil War, half the sugar consumed in America was produced in Louisiana.

33

WRANGLE A CRAWFISH BOIL INVITE

WHAT'S THE DEAL? Few things say "New Orleans" like a crawfish boil. Crawfish season runs from mid-January to early July. The crawfish, potatoes, and corn are boiled up and thrown down on a newspaper-covered picnic table all at once while family and new friends gather to eat, drink, and shoot the sh#t. No invite? Host your own.

DO IT IF: You want to hang with strangers and suck the brains out of crawfish.

SKIP IT IF: You carry an EpiPen for your shellfish allergy.

LOCAL ADVICE: Buy crawfish at Bevi Seafood Co. *(236 N. Carrollton Ave. beviseafoodco.com)* and take them to City Park. Three pounds per person is a serving.

I DID IT: ☐ #nolabucket #mudbugs

DID YOU KNOW?

Crawfish, also known as mudbugs or crawdads, are the official crustacean of Louisiana. The proper technique for consuming one is to twist it in half, pinch the tail, eat the meat, and suck the juice out of the head.

34

FIND IGNATIUS J. REILLY

WHAT'S THE DEAL? The Hyatt Centric French Quarter *(800 Iberville St., Canal St. side)* boasts a statue of the eccentric antihero from "A Confederacy of Dunces" waiting beneath the clock. Reilly is often touted as a modern-day Don Quixote, and loyal fans of the cult classic make a pilgrimage to the location for a photo with him.

DO IT IF: You are a fan of John Kennedy Toole

SKIP IT IF: Your 'statue' of limitations has expired.

LOCAL ADVICE: Grab a "Lucky Dog" *(several locations)* in Reilly's honor. They are the inspiration for the "Paradise Hot Dogs" in the novel.

I DID IT: ☐ #nolabucket #duncesdance

DID YOU KNOW?

A Confederacy of Dunces is famous for its rich depiction of New Orleans and the city's dialects. It was published posthumously in 1980, 11 years after the author's suicide.

35

WALK IN A SOLDIER'S FOOTSTEPS

WHAT'S THE DEAL? Designated by Congress as America's official museum about World War II, The National World War II Museum *(945 Magazine St., nationalww2museum.org)* documents the trials and tribulations our men and women in uniform faced in the war that changed the world.

DO IT IF: You want to learn about this war from a soldier's perspective.

SKIP IT IF: You already got bombed on Bourbon Street.

LOCAL ADVICE: Plan to spend the day here. There are many exhibits, and if you stick around until Happy Hour, you can catch two for one at the Museum bar. Do not miss *Beyond All Boundaries*, a 4-D film experience narrated by Tom Hanks.

I DID IT: ☐ #nolabucket #soldieron

DID YOU KNOW?

The museum's collection includes over 9000 personal accounts of the war and more than 250,000 artifacts.

36

THROW BEADS FROM A BALCONY

WHAT'S THE DEAL? Beads are currency in New Orleans, and it doesn't have to be Mardi Gras for people in the French Quarter to seek them out. Each weekend, people look to the balconies on Bourbon Street for beads. Bourbon Bars like "The Swamp" *(516 Bourbon St., bourbon-swamp.com)* welcome thrill seekers on their balcony nightly. Go ahead and toss them a strand.

DO IT IF: You have a hotel room with a balcony on Bourbon Street.

SKIP IT IF: You feel like a boob tossing strings of plastic.

LOCAL ADVICE: Go to a Mardi Gras supply store like Plush Appeal *(2811 Toulouse St., mardigrasspot.com)* to get your beads. Their prices are significantly lower than the stores selling them on Bourbon Street.

I DID IT: ☐ #nolabucket #beadyeyed

DID YOU KNOW?

Glass beads were first thrown out by Mardi Gras krewes in the early 1800s. During parades in Carnival season, you don't have to do anything to get beads, except speak the popular request, "Throw me something, Mister!" In 2019, 93,000 pounds of plastic beads were recovered from New Orleans storm drains.

37

DRINK A
DRIVE-THRU DAIQUIRI

WHAT'S THE DEAL? Louisiana has some of the most relaxed liquor laws in the country. Exhibit A: drive-thru daiquiri shops. Swing by New Orleans' Original Daiquiris *(3637 General Degaulle Dr., nolaoriginal.com)* if you need more evidence.

DO IT IF: You're a fan of the backseat brain freeze.

SKIP IT IF: You are the designated driver.

LOCAL ADVICE: Try a 190 Octane. No floater required.

I DID IT: ☐ #nolabucket #drivethrudaiquiri

DID YOU KNOW?

You can have a daiquiri in the car, but you can't have a straw in it, or it is classified as an open container. On Bourbon Street, you can walk with a drink in your hand 24/7.

38

GET LOST IN THE SWAMP

WHAT'S THE DEAL? Audubon Zoo *(6500 Magazine St., audubonnatureinstitute.org)* is a New Orleans treasure. A multitude of exhibits feature animals from around the world in natural habitats. The Louisiana Swamp exhibit examines the relationship between Cajun people, plants, and animals of the swamp. It is one of the most popular attractions for both locals and visitors.

DO IT IF: You like Swamp People.

SKIP IT IF: You have a reptile dysfunction.

LOCAL ADVICE: Take the Saint Charles Streetcar and enjoy a walk through Audubon Park to the zoo entrance, about a mile. There is a shuttle where you get off the streetcar if you're feeling lazy.

I DID IT: ☐ #nolabucket #swampass

DID YOU KNOW?

Rougarou is a legendary Cajun swamp monster and shapeshifter. It is described as a creature with a human body and the head of a wolf.

39

TAKE A CLASS IN GLITTEROLOGY

WHAT'S THE DEAL? Make your own glittery souvenir. Numerous workshops teach you to master glitter art and create one-of-a-kind masterpieces like the collectible shoes thrown from the floats in the Muses Mardi Gras parade. Check out NOLA Craft Culture *(127 S. Solomon St., nolacraftculture.com)* for days and times. Advance booking is recommended.

DO IT IF: You're crafty.

SKIP IT IF: You have a thing for eating paste.

LOCAL ADVICE: Before you go, get some inspiration from Carnival themed websites like *kreweofmuses.org.*

I DID IT: ☐ #nolabucket #glittersisgold

DID YOU KNOW?

Collectible throws are some of the most coveted souvenirs from New Orleans. Muses shoes have sold on eBay for over $150 in the past. Other popular throws include Zulu coconuts and purses from the Krewe of Nyx.

40

TIP YOUR FAVORITE BUSKER

WHAT'S THE DEAL? New Orleans is a haven for street performers, with impromptu shows erupting across the French Quarter day and night. Silver Guys? Jugglers? Magicians? Troubadours? Find your favorite, enjoy the show, and make their day by tossing some cash in their hat.

DO IT IF: You like win-win situations.

SKIP IT IF: You think there are tracking chips in currency, and you only use Bitcoin.

LOCAL ADVICE: Prime busking time starts just before sunset. Start in Jackson Square *(701 Decatur St.)*. From the Chartres Street side, walk-up Pirate's Alley to Royal Street to experience some of the more interesting performers.

I DID IT: ☐ #nolabucket #buskamove

DID YOU KNOW?

Jackson Square is the heart of the French Quarter and remains a showcase for artists of all mediums, including street performers. Civil War widows once sold paintings in the square to support their families.

41

WATCH A MOVIE IN A PARK

WHAT'S THE DEAL? Outdoor Movies can be found at parks throughout New Orleans. The outdoor spaces on the Lafitte Greenway are some of the most popular venues and primary locations for the New Orleans Film Festival. Check Eventbrite *(eventbrite.com)* for upcoming showings in town.

DO IT IF: You are a movie buff.

SKIP IT IF: You like to watch movies in the buff.

LOCAL ADVICE: Buy festival chairs at a local convenience store, or use a blanket if that's your thing. Don't forget the insect repellant.

I DID IT: ☐ #nolabucket #actionpark

DID YOU KNOW?

New Orleans has over 2,000 acres of public green space, two major parks, and 200 smaller parks and squares.

42

THROW A STRIKE AT ROCK 'N' BOWL

WHAT'S THE DEAL? New Orleans Rock 'n' Bowl *(3016 S Carrollton Ave., rocknbowl.com)* is a locally driven institution with 18 bowling lanes, live music by local luminaries, a dance floor, and a bar menu with Creole-inspired fare. You don't have to bowl here to have a good time.

DO IT IF: Local institutions are right up your alley.

SKIP IT IF: You'd prefer to strike out on a different adventure.

LOCAL ADVICE: Go on a Thursday for Zydeco Music Night.

I DID IT: ☐ #nolabucket #rocknbowl

DID YOU KNOW?

Rock 'n' Bowl has been featured in National Geographic, Life Magazine, USA Today, and Rolling Stone.

43

TASTE LOCAL SPIRITS

WHAT'S THE DEAL? Seven Three Distilling Co. *(301 N. Claiborne Ave., seventhreedistilling.com)* celebrates the 73 neighborhoods of New Orleans by crafting distinctive spirits made with locally farmed ingredients. Their simple goal, in their own words, "To capture the unmistakable flavor of this one-of-a-kind American city by crafting spirits with a sense of place." They are open for tours and spirit tastings daily.

DO IT IF: You are a fan of 'still' life.

SKIP IT IF: You just became friends with Bill W.

LOCAL ADVICE: Try the Marigny Moonshine for a New Orleans kick.

I DID IT: ☐ #nolabucket #stilllife

DID YOU KNOW?

Seven Three Distilling Co. produces rum, gin, whiskey, vodka, and moonshine.

44

LEARN TO BOUNCE & TWERK

WHAT'S THE DEAL? Bounce music is a New Orleans hip hop music style that originated in the city's housing projects. Book a lesson with Moe Joe of Moe Joe Gallery fame (*themoejoe.com, datmoejoe@gmail.com*), and you can learn the moves to bounce and twerk.

DO IT IF: You want to work on your twerk.

SKIP IT IF: Your back's out of whack.

LOCAL ADVICE: Follow "Big Freedia" on social media. She does live concerts from her living room, as well as cooking demonstrations.

I DID IT: ☐ #nolabucket #junkinthetrunk

DID YOU KNOW?

Bounce music is characterized by a call-and-response style and Mardi Gras Indian chants and challenges. New Orleans's very own "Queen of Bounce," Big Freedia, brought bounce music into the mainstream.

45

ANTIQUE ON ROYAL STREET

WHAT'S THE DEAL? Founded in 1718, New Orleans has a lot of history under its belt and no shortage of antiques. You can find the best of the best in the shops along Royal Street in the French Quarter.

DO IT IF: You like searching for treasure.

SKIP IT IF: You own an IKEA store.

LOCAL ADVICE: Check out M.S. Rau *(622 Royal St., rauantiques.com)* for an impressive collection of antique jewelry.

I DID IT: ☐ #nolabucket #junkinthetrunk

DID YOU KNOW?

New Orleans for some time in the 1800s was the richest city per capita in the country. Combine that with 300 years of history, and you have an antique scene worth exploring for amateurs and diehards alike, with something for everyone and every budget.

46

TAKE A PHOTO AT
THE FLAMING FOUNTAIN

WHAT'S THE DEAL? Who says fire and water don't mix? Pat O'Brien's *(718 St. Peter, patobriens.com)* courtyard has an iconic flaming fountain that is interesting to watch—it's worth snapping a pic when you stop in for a famous Hurricane. Do it on your first drink. The Hurricanes can creep up on you.

DO IT IF: You have a burning desire.

SKIP IT IF: You are a vampire and don't show up in photographs.

LOCAL ADVICE: Try a mint julep instead of a hurricane at Pat's. You won't be disappointed.

I DID IT: ☐ #nolabucket #firewater

DID YOU KNOW?

During prohibition, Pat O'Brien's operated as Mr. O'Brien's Club Tipperary. Guests used the password "storm's brewing" to gain entrance.

47

CREATE AN
OUTLANDISH HEADDRESS

WHAT'S THE DEAL? Headdresses have been a part of the New Orleans costume scene since Governor Bienville wore a powdered white wig in the 18th century. The outlandish, colorful accessories are a Carnival fashion statement celebrated all year long. Several individuals and businesses offer classes in headdress making; One of our favorites is artist Ellen Macomber. She hosts wintertime workshops in her gallery. *(The Brainard House, 2126 Brainard St. ellenmacomber.com/collections/workshops)*

DO IT IF: You're tired of people making eye contact when they talk to you.

SKIP IT IF: You prefer your head naked.

LOCAL ADVICE: Bring cherished trinkets from home to enhance your creation.

I DID IT: ☐ #nolabucket #headdress

DID YOU KNOW?

Wigs and headpieces are a major part of any self-respecting New Orleanian's closet. Several events each year require a headdress for participation.

48

LEARN TO CAJUN TWO-STEP

WHAT'S THE DEAL? Cajun two-step is a popular dance brought to Louisiana by the Cajuns - displaced French-speaking Acadians. They moved to New Orleans from Canada. It is the most common dance at Zydeco concerts and festivals.

DO IT IF: If you want to look good on the dance floor at the next Fais do-do.

SKIP IT IF: You can't rise to the o' Cajun.

LOCAL ADVICE: The Tigermen Den *(3113 Royal St., thetigermenden.com)* in the Bywater neighborhood has free Cajun two-step lessons seasonally. Check their Insta for up-to-date info.

I DID IT: ☐ #nolabucket #cajundance

DID YOU KNOW?

The three primary dances of Cajun music are the Cajun two-step, the Cajun jitterbug, and waltz.

49

STAND UNDER THE BALCONY WHERE ELVIS SANG

WHAT'S THE DEAL? The opening scene of 1958's *King Creole* has Elvis Presley singing about crawfish on a New Orleans balcony. Elvis fans come from around the world to gaze up at this sacred place and take a pic to prove they walked in the shadow of the King.

DO IT IF: You have a TCB flash tattoo.

SKIP IT IF: Your only king is drinking.

LOCAL ADVICE: *1018 Royal Street* is the address. Watch the opening scene on YouTube or stream the song performed by Elvis Presley and Kitty White.

I DID IT: ☐ #nolabucket #kingcreole

DID YOU KNOW?

King Creole was Elvis Presley's third film and the last picture he made before entering the U.S. Army. To shoot the movie, Elvis was given a sixty-day deferment.

50

MEET SAINT EXPEDITE

WHAT'S THE DEAL? Our Lady of Guadalupe Church *(411 N Rampart St., judeshrine.com)* is home to Saint Expedite's statue—Expedite is the patron Saint of speeding things up and removing procrastination. Some say he was a Roman Centurion who converted to Christianity. Another story says the figure was discovered in a box on a dock by non-English speaking nuns and the box was simply marked "EXPEDITE."

DO IT IF: You keep putting things off.

SKIP IT IF: You'll get to it on your next visit.

LOCAL ADVICE: Bring Sara Lee pound cake as an offering. Buy a St. Expedite candle at Island of Salvation Botanica *(2372 St. Claude Ave., islandofsalvationbotanica.com)*. Burn it when you need a speedy resolution to a legal problem.

I DID IT: ☐   #nolabucket #rushordersaint

DID YOU KNOW?

Our Lady of Guadalupe Church was initially built as a mortuary chapel for victims of yellow fever. It is the oldest surviving church building in New Orleans.

51

SAVOR A TRADITIONAL PO-BOY

WHAT'S THE DEAL? The po-boy is a traditional Louisiana sandwich made with meat or fried seafood served on a New Orleans French bread famous for its crisp crust and fluffy center. Parkway Bakery & Tavern *(538 Hagan Ave., parkwaypoorboys.com)* is a local favorite.

DO IT IF: You want to eat like a local.

SKIP IT IF: You don't like to get messy when you eat.

LOCAL ADVICE: "Dressed" means lettuce, tomato, pickles, and mayo. The Peacemaker is an oyster and shrimp combo served around New Orleans. Try the Parkway Surf & Turf for a shrimp and roast beef delight. Dressed, of course.

I DID IT: ☐ #nolabucket #pogirl

DID YOU KNOW?

The name "po-boy" is thought to have been coined by a couple of streetcar conductors turned restaurateurs during a transit strike in the early 1900s.

52

WALK THE DOGS
AT VILLALOBOS

WHAT'S THE DEAL? Featured in a reality series on Animal Planet, Villalobos Rescue Center *(4525 N. Galvez St., vrcpitbull.com)* specializes in pitbulls and hounds. They need volunteers to help walk the adoptable dogs at their New Orleans location daily.

DO IT IF: You miss your dog and want to help others.

SKIP IT IF: You have fleas.

LOCAL ADVICE: Dog walks are every Saturday from 1-3 pm, and they also need "Kennel Cleaners" daily from 10 am to 12 pm. Please email to reserve a spot at volunteer@vrcpitbull.com.

I DID IT: ☐   #nolabucket #pitstop

DID YOU KNOW?

Villalobos' rescue dogs and pups were featured in the 2021 Dog Bowl and Puppy Bowl.

53

EXPERIENCE A DRAG BRUNCH

WHAT'S THE DEAL? New Orleans is famous for drag queens and brunch. Several establishments have combined these two elements to create an unforgettable brunch experience. Check out The Country Club *(634 Louisa St., thecountryclubneworleans.com)* for one of the longest-running drag brunches in town.

DO IT IF: You would like some Gloria Gaynor with your omelet.

SKIP IT IF: You are uncomfortable with your sexuality.

LOCAL ADVICE: Bring a fist full of dollars. The drag queens love it when you make it rain.

I DID IT: [ ] #nolabucket #dragbrunch

DID YOU KNOW?

New Orleans is an epicenter of drag culture. Gretna native Roy Haylock, aka Bianca Del Rio, won RuPaul's Drag Race's sixth season.

54

DIG DEGAS

WHAT'S THE DEAL? Edgar Degas is one of the top French Impressionist painters. He spent a year in New Orleans from 1872-1873 and honed the techniques that established his reputation. The stately mansion where he stayed has been preserved as a B&B and Degas House Museum *(2306 Esplanade Ave., degashouse.com)*

DO IT IF: You like great first impressions.

SKIP IT IF: Impressionist paintings look like splattered paint to you.

LOCAL ADVICE: Keep the theme going with lunch at nearby Café Degas. The French Onion soup is magnifique! There are also works by Degas at NOMA.

I DID IT: ☐   #nolabucket #vivalasdegas

DID YOU KNOW?

This house is the only known home or studio of Degas that is open to the public. He created 18 paintings and four drawings depicting his New Orleans family members here.

55

CROSS THE PONTCHARTRAIN BRIDGE

WHAT'S THE DEAL? The Lake Pontchartrain Causeway is a 23.83-mile long bridge connecting Metairie and Mandeville across Lake Pontchartrain. It is the longest bridge over a continuous body of water in the world.

DO IT IF: You like record-breaking bridges.

SKIP IT IF: You refuse to pay tolls or suffer from gephyrophobia.

LOCAL ADVICE: Stop for Chinese food at Trey Yuen on the Northshore. *(600 N. Causeway Blvd., Mandeville, treyyuen.com)*

I DID IT: ☐   #nolabucket #longestbridge

DID YOU KNOW?

In 2011, Guinness named the Jiaozhou Bay Bridge in China the longest bridge over water, causing controversy in Louisiana. This led to two designations. The Pontchartrain Causeway remained the longest bridge over a continuous water body. The bridge in China, crossing over both water and rice paddies, was awarded the longest aggregate bridge accolade.

56

LUNCH AT
THE HERMES BAR

WHAT'S THE DEAL? Antoine's *(713 St. Louis St., antoines.com)* is the oldest family-run restaurant in the United States. It opened in 1840 and is the birthplace of Oysters Rockefeller. Inside Antoine's is the opulent Hermes Bar. Stop in for lunch and taste the history.

DO IT IF: You want to experience the pearl of the Quarter.

SKIP IT IF: Oysters make you horny, and you are traveling solo.

LOCAL ADVICE: Ask a maître d' if you can see the Mardi Gras memorabilia on the second floor. They have one of the best collections around. Antoine's soufflé potatoes are a local favorite.

I DID IT: ☐ #nolabucket #hermesbar

DID YOU KNOW?

Jules Alciatore, Antoine's son, named a new dish Oysters Rockefeller because of the richness of the sauce.

57

JOIN IN A
REAL SECOND LINE

WHAT'S THE DEAL? The Second Line is a New Orleans tradition where people parade through the streets behind a band to celebrate a person or occasion. If you've already made a wish at the Second Line fountain, it's time to try the real deal. You don't need an invitation. Just join in.

DO IT IF: You love dancing in the streets.

SKIP IT IF: You're on your third line already.

LOCAL ADVICE: *WWOZ.org* publishes a list showing the days and locations of the real Second Lines put on by Social Aid and Pleasure Clubs. In season, they typically take place on Sundays. Bring a handkerchief to wave in the air.

I DID IT: ☐ #nolabucket #buckjumping

DID YOU KNOW?

Second Lines have their history with enslaved Africans and became formally organized when something called "Social Aid and Pleasure Clubs" were created. These SAPCs began providing community help for people of color refused coverage by white insurance companies.

58

FIND A SHAKOR

WHAT'S THE DEAL? Murals and street art are part of the fabric that weaves the soul of New Orleans. Shakor created the art on this book's cover and is a favorite local artist known for vibrant murals depicting New Orleans life. Stop by Galley Cayenne, "Fine Art with the Spice of New Orleans," *(702 Decatur St., next to Café du Monde, gallerycayenne.com)* to see more of his works, and then set out on a street art safari to see if you can spot which murals around New Orleans are his.

DO IT IF: You want to see how the town is painted before you paint the town.

SKIP IT IF: Your father is Banksy.

LOCAL ADVICE: Try the Marigny and Bywater neighborhoods for a self-propelled safari. Start at the Healing Center *(2372 St. Claude Ave.)*

I DID IT: ☐ #nolabucket #moreshakor

DID YOU KNOW?

New Orleans has more than 140 murals located throughout the city. The controversial English artist "Banksy" was here in 2008 and left 18 works of public art, though only a few remain.

59

COOL OFF WITH A SNO-BALL

WHAT'S THE DEAL? The combination of shaved ice and a flavored syrup has been elevated to an art form in New Orleans. Baltimore claims to have invented this treat, but it wasn't until the invention of the electric ice shaver in New Orleans in the 1930s that the real Sno-Ball made its appearance.

DO IT IF: You're feeling hot and bothered.

SKIP IT IF: Aaag! Brain freeze!

LOCAL ADVICE: Hit Sno-La *(8108 Hampson St., snolasnowballs.com)* and try a cheesecake-stuffed snowball with sweetened condensed milk. Hours vary seasonally.

I DID IT: ☐ #nolabucket #snoballschance

DID YOU KNOW?

The New Orleans Sno-Ball's ice texture is much more delicate and soft than the Baltimore version. It resembles fresh snow.

60

PEDAL AN ART BIKE

WHAT'S THE DEAL? An art bike is any rideable bike modified for creative purposes. They are a staple of New Orleans parades. The Krewe of Kolossos *(kolossos.org)* has a fleet of colorful bikes decked out in papier-mâché, and they are happy to help you get on a parade route.

DO IT IF: You were born to be wild.

SKIP IT IF: You were born to be mild.

LOCAL ADVICE: St. Patrick's Day parade is a blast if your trip lines up.

I DID IT: ☐ #nolabucket #artmyride

DID YOU KNOW?

Katrina Brees' Krewe of Kolossos *(kolossoss.org/art-bikes)* popularized the art bike in New Orleans. Their menagerie includes an entire art bike zoo with many different animals.

61

KAYAK THE BAYOU

WHAT'S THE DEAL? Bayou St. John has been an important waterway since the Europeans established a colony on the Mississippi banks. The bayou is a refreshing dose of nature, and its shorelines are a favorite with locals. There are several kayak rental companies in New Orleans. Try Kayak-Iti-Yat *(3494 Esplanade Ave., kayakitiyat.com)* for a guided bayou tour.

DO IT IF: You would like the bayou by you.

SKIP IT IF: You have a fear of being eaten by alligators.

LOCAL ADVICE: Leave an offering to Marie Laveau on the Magnolia Bridge.

I DID IT: ☐ #nolabucket #bluebayou

DID YOU KNOW?

Voodoo practitioners hold rituals along Bayou St. John's banks, including a St. John's Eve ceremony on the Magnolia Bridge.

62

LEARN LOCAL COCKTAIL HISTORY

WHAT'S THE DEAL? Several famous cocktails were created in New Orleans, one of the most famous being a sugary libation including rye whiskey, absinthe, and Peychaud's Bitters called the Sazerac. The Sazerac is the official drink of New Orleans, and claims to be the first American cocktail. Take a tour at the Sazerac House *(101 Magazine St., sazerachouse.com)* for fascinating cocktail history.

DO IT IF: You want to drink in some history.

SKIP IT IF: You 're not willing to give it a shot.

LOCAL ADVICE: Drink a Sazerac at The Roosevelt New Orleans' Sazerac Bar *(130 Roosevelt Way, therooseveltneworleans.com)*.

I DID IT: ☐   #nolabucket #drinkinghistory

DID YOU KNOW?

It took a Federal agent just 37 seconds to buy a cocktail in New Orleans during prohibition. He asked his cab driver where a fellow could buy a drink in this town, and the cab driver sold him one, making the Big Easy the "'easiest" city to buy an illegal drink in the United States.

63

LISTEN TO
THE STREETS SING

WHAT'S THE DEAL? The diversity of music emanating from the streets of New Orleans is second to none. An overlooked gem in the city occurs the moment two musical genres blend between competing street corners to create their own Crescent City symphony. It is the unofficial soundtrack of the Big Easy. Stroll Royal Street after dinner for a taste of the magic.

DO IT IF: New Orleans is music to your ears.

SKIP IT IF: You are on your way home from ear replacement surgery.

LOCAL ADVICE: Catch some authentic New Orleans jams with Doreen Ketchens outside Rouses Market *(701 Royal St.)* most weekends for a taste of clarinet magic.

I DID IT: ☐ #nolabucket #allears

DID YOU KNOW?

Rod Stewart, Tracy Chapman, and B.B. King all got their start playing music in the streets.

64

DANCE WITH
A MOTLEY KREWE

WHAT'S THE DEAL? A krewe is a New Orleans social organization that hosts parades and balls during Carnival season. Many host community charity events all year. Several krewes offer visitors the opportunity to attend practice with them to learn various dances. Try it for a behind the scenes taste of Carnival.

DO IT IF: You have dance fever.

SKIP IT IF: You have a fever.

LOCAL ADVICE: NOLA Chorus Girls *(nolachorusgirls.com)* teach original choreographies to New Orleans music. No audition required.

I DID IT: ☐ #nolabucket #motleykrewe

DID YOU KNOW?

More than 60 active dancing/marching krewes exist in New Orleans, including the Pussyfooters, the 610 Stompers, the Bearded Oysters, and the Rolling Elvi.

65

SIT BENEATH THE TREE OF LIFE

WHAT'S THE DEAL? The Tree of Life *(East Dr.)* is a sprawling live oak in Audubon Park *(6500 Magazine St.)* The Live Oak Society estimates it to be between 100 and 500 years old. The tree is suitable for climbing and even better for photo ops and pondering life's mysteries.

DO IT IF: You want to go out on a limb.

SKIP IT IF: You don't want to turn over a new leaf.

LOCAL ADVICE: Look over the zoo wall, and you might see giraffes. Walk the nearby meditation labyrinth to set the tone.

I DID IT: ☐ #nolabucket #treeoflife

DID YOU KNOW?

The tree's official name is the Étienne de Bore Oak, named after the first mayor of New Orleans. He is mostly credited with making sugarcane a feasible cash crop in the Crescent City.

66

PLAY IN
MUSIC BOX VILLAGE

WHAT'S THE DEAL? If unique musical instruments had sex with funky Cajun cottages, their babies would be The Music Box Village *(4557 N. Rampart St., musicboxvillage.com)*. These interactive, outdoor, musical art installations create a playground of sound that is great for all ages.

DO IT IF: Get it on, bang a gong is your motto.

SKIP IT IF: Large musical instruments intimidate you.

LOCAL ADVICE: Grab some wine and cheese around the corner at local favorite Bacchanal *(600 Poland Ave.)* after your visit.

I DID IT: ☐ #nolabucket #whatsinthebox

DID YOU KNOW?

The Music Box Village has been home to concerts by some of the top musicians in New Orleans, including Grammy award-winning artists like Ricky Lee Jones and the Lost Bayou Ramblers.

67

SIP & SWIM
IN A SECRET POOL

WHAT'S THE DEAL? A charming Creole mansion with a restaurant and hidden pool is hidden away in the historic Bywater neighborhood— the Country Club has been called "New Orleans' best-kept secret." The Country Club *(634 Louisa St., thecountryclubneworleans.com)* is a perfect escape for lunch, cocktails, and a dip with the locals. 21 and older only.

DO IT IF: You want to make a splash at a local hideaway.

SKIP IT IF: You pee in pools.

LOCAL ADVICE: Go on a rainy day. If it's raining, it's happy hour.

I DID IT: ☐ #nolabucket #secretswim

DID YOU KNOW?

Built in 1884, the Country Club is an Italianate Raised Center Hall Cottage. This architectural style became common in the South during the early 1800s.

68

SEE FAMOUS MOVIE SITES

WHAT'S THE DEAL? Filmmakers have set their sights on New Orleans since celluloid was invented. The volume of productions earned New Orleans the nickname "Hollywood South." Original NOLA Historic Tours *(tourneworleans.com)* can arrange a private walking or driving tour of famous on-location sites used in Benjamin Button, Interview with the Vampire, and NCIS: New Orleans, to name a few

DO IT IF: You want to say you've seen the scene of the scene.

SKIP IT IF: You're from Hollywood.

LOCAL ADVICE: Keep your eyes peeled on St. Ann Street between Royal and Bourbon. The NCIS headquarters is hidden there. Behind closed doors, of course.

I DID IT: ☐ #nolabucket #hollywoodsouth

DID YOU KNOW?

Over 180 feature films have been shot at least partially in New Orleans, including *12 Years a Slave*, *King Creole*, and *Interview with the Vampire*.

69

MUNCH A MUFFULETTA ON THE MISSISSIPPI

WHAT'S THE DEAL? The Muffuletta is a New Orleans sandwich made with sesame bread, salami, ham, mortadella, provolone, Swiss, and olive salad, made popular by Sicilian immigrants who came to New Orleans after the Civil War. Get one where they were first created and enjoy it on the banks of the nearby Mississippi.

DO IT IF: You like your sandwiches the bigger, the better.

SKIP IT IF: You are allergic to olives.

LOCAL ADVICE: The first muffuletta was created in 1906 at Central Grocery & Deli *(923 Decatur St., centralgrocery.com)* They are rebuilding after severe damage sustained in Hurricane Ida, but in the meantime, check their website to find out where you can buy their original sandwiches all around town. Our suggestion: right next door at Sidney's Wine Cellar (917 Decatur St.) Garb a Barq's Root Beer to wash it down and cross the street to the river.

I DID IT: ☐ #nolabucket #muffmunch

DID YOU KNOW?

There were so many Sicilians in the French Quarter that at one time it was called "Il Piccollo Palermo!" - "Little Palermo."

70

CHECK OUT
AN ART MARKET

WHAT'S THE DEAL? Art markets are a great place to find meaningful gifts and souvenirs that were not produced in a plastic factory overseas. They abound in this city of creativity, and every purchase is an investment in part of New Orleans' charm. Check out the Disco Warehouse *(3101 Tchoupitoulas St. discowarehouse.net)* every other Saturday.

DO IT IF: You want to give your dog-sitter a gift they'll dig.

SKIP IT IF: You spent all your souvenir money on crack.

LOCAL ADVICE: *Artsneworleans.org* has a monthly listing of markets, including one-of-a-kind pop-ups.

I DID IT: ☐   #nolabucket #artinheart

DID YOU KNOW?

New Orleans' cultural industries accounted for 37,793 jobs in 2016. Illustrators, painters, jewelers, sculptors, mosaic artists and potters are just a sample of the creative individuals that call New Orleans home.

71

FIND A FESTIVAL

WHAT'S THE DEAL? With over 130 different festivals every year, New Orleans is a strong contender for the "Festival Capital of the World" title. That's roughly one festival every three days, so finding one should be a breeze.

DO IT IF: You're feeling festive.

SKIP IT IF: You have agoraphobia.

LOCAL ADVICE: Find event calendars online from Gambit *(nola.com/gambit)* or Where Y'at *(whereyat.com)*. Grab a free print copy of each when you arrive. They are distributed all over town.

I DID IT: ☐ #nolabucket #feelingfestive

DID YOU KNOW?

New Orleans Jazz & Heritage Festival attracts some of the biggest names in entertainment. The Rolling Stones, Elton John, Fleetwood Mac, and Bruce Springsteen are a few of the acts that have graced the stages at this popular festival.

72

MEET THE QUEEN
OF BOURBON STREET

WHAT'S THE DEAL? One of our most beloved New Orleans street performers is the ageless Mamie Marie *(facebook.com/silverfoxxnola)*. She is known as the Silver Foxx and the Queen of Bourbon Street. You can find her riding her blinged-out tricycle down the famed street most nights, with her music jamming, spreading love and cheer. Say hello and take a selfie with the Queen.

DO IT IF: You want to feel like the king of the world.

SKIP IT IF: You were expecting this adventure to be about Freddie Mercury.

LOCAL ADVICE: Don't be mean. Tip the Queen.

I DID IT: ☐ #nolabucket #royals

DID YOU KNOW?

Bourbon Street extends thirteen blocks from Canal Street to Esplanade Avenue.

73

HAVE A DRINK AT
THE COLUMNS HOTEL

WHAT'S THE DEAL? Designed by one of New Orleans' great architects and built in 1883, the Columns Hotel *(3811 St. Charles Ave., thecolumns.com)* was once the private home of a wealthy tobacco merchant. Sipping a mint julep on the iconic veranda and watching streetcars go by is a perfect way to while away an hour, or two, or three.

DO IT IF: You're feeling a bit Ionic.

SKIP IT IF: You're a big Doric.

LOCAL ADVICE: Take the streetcar. It will drop you close by.

I DID IT: ☐ #nolabucket #bigdoric

DID YOU KNOW?

The Columns is a favorite of many Hollywood directors. *American Horror Story: Coven,* and the movies *Pretty Baby* and *12 Years a Slave* filmed scenes here.

74

EXPLORE THE CITIES OF THE DEAD

WHAT'S THE DEAL? The water table in New Orleans makes in-ground burials problematic. As a result, above ground mausoleums and tombs dominate the cemeteries, creating "cities of the dead" – a term coined by author Mark Twain. There are several worth exploring throughout the city.

DO IT IF: You are dying to get in.

SKIP IT IF: You are a necrophiliac.

LOCAL ADVICE: Enlist a tour guide and discover the stories of the people inside the tombs. *(luckybeantours.com)* Metairie Cemetery is an excellent place to bring a picnic lunch.

I DID IT: ☐ #nolabucket #ghostfarms

DID YOU KNOW?

Established in 1789, Saint Louis Cemetery No. 1 is the oldest and most famous cemetery in New Orleans.

75

HIRE A POET

WHAT'S THE DEAL? Poetry is not just for lovelorn Lotharios, and there are numerous poets for hire in New Orleans waiting to prove this. Simply head to Royal Street on a nice day, select a poet, give them a topic, and watch the magic unfold. They are easy to spot, as they are the only ones perched on the sidewalk with an old school typewriter. The results will delight you.

DO IT IF: You want to be the star of a poem.

SKIP IT IF: You are the man from Nantucket.

LOCAL ADVICE: Put it in a thrift shop frame for a unique souvenir.

I DID IT: ☐ #nolabucket #manfromnantucket

DID YOU KNOW?

Tennessee Williams, William Faulkner, Charles Bukowski, John Kennedy Toole, F. Scott Fitzgerald, Lillian Hellman, and Mark Twain all found inspiration on the streets of the French Quarter.

76

GUSSY UP IN A MARDI GRAS COSTUME

WHAT'S THE DEAL? New Orleans residents love to dress up in costume, and you can do it too. Visit the Mardi Gras Museum of Costume and Culture *(1010 Conti St., themardigrasmuseum.com)* and spend some time in their costume closet living out your Mardi Gras fantasies, and become King or Queen for the day.

DO IT IF: You have a thing for satin and tiaras.

SKIP IT IF: You have a thing for Satan and tiaras.

LOCAL ADVICE: Go during Carnival for free King Cake.

I DID IT: ☐ #nolabucket #mardigrasmagic

DID YOU KNOW?

Many New Orleans masks trace their origins to the masks worn by Carnival revelers in Venice, Italy.

77

CATCH A PEEP SHOW

WHAT'S THE DEAL? The AllWays Lounge & Cabaret *(2240 St. Claude Ave., theallwayslounge.net)* has some of the best burlesque performers around. Experience a live, private peep show at their Backstage Boutique. Just step behind the curtain and get a peek at what's behind the glass.

DO IT IF: You want to keep abreast of the New Orleans burlesque scene.

SKIP IT IF: Boobs make you blush.

LOCAL ADVICE: Purchase tokens at the bar. Tip performers through the slot.

I DID IT: ☐ #nolabucket #callmetom

DID YOU KNOW?

The AllWays Lounge has been a safe space for male-identifying, female-identifying, people of color, and queer performers for over 11 years. This venue is one of the original New Orleans alternative theaters.

78

CHANT WITH HARE KRISHNAS

WHAT'S THE DEAL? The Hare Krishna movement is often lampooned in pop culture, preventing many people from discovering the solid spiritual practices built around the Hindu Lord Krishna's teaching. Visit the ISKCON New Orleans temple *(2936 Esplanade Ave., iskconnola.org)* for a unique taste of the Krishna culture.

DO IT IF: You like learning about spirituality.

SKIP IT IF: You can't chant.

LOCAL ADVICE: Go for the Love Feast on Sunday from 6 pm - 8 pm. Vedic wisdom and a free vegetarian dinner.

I DID IT: ☐ #nolabucket #harekrishna

DID YOU KNOW?

The International Society for Krishna Consciousness *(ISKCON)'s* goal is to introduce all people of the world to self-realization and God-consciousness in order to derive the highest benefit of spiritual understanding, unity, and peace.

79

FRIDAY LUNCH
AT GALATOIRE'S

WHAT'S THE DEAL? Galatoire's *(209 Bourbon St., galatoires.com)* is a classic New Orleans restaurant has been wowing diners with their French-Creole fare since 1905. Their Friday lunch is one of the hottest tickets in town, with fantastic food, a convivial setting, and countless celebrations.

DO IT IF: You like the hotspots.

SKIP IT IF: You don't like waiting in line.

LOCAL ADVICE: To sit in the coveted downstairs dining room, arrive early in the morning, or hire someone to line-sit for you. Try the Café Brûlot.

I DID IT: ☐ #nolabucket #feastoffriends

DID YOU KNOW?

People get paid to line-sit in New Orleans. At Galatoire's, lines for Friday lunch start forming as early as 4 am.

80

SCORE A HOLE-IN-ONE

WHAT'S THE DEAL? City Putt *(33 Dreyfous Dr., neworleanscitypark.com/in-the-park/city-putt)* is a charming miniature golf complex inside City Park, themed after iconic and cultural aspects of New Orleans and Louisiana. It's the perfect place to nail the hole-in-one that evades you on the big courses.

DO IT IF: You want to putt around New Orleans.

SKIP IT IF: You want to putt around your hotel room.

LOCAL ADVICE: Play two rounds. The second one is discounted. No cheating.

I DID IT: ☐ #nolabucket #iheartbingle

DID YOU KNOW?

Mr. Bingle is a large snowman with an ice cream cone hat who helps Santa. People in New Orleans have a strange obsession with the creature. He can be found stalking golfers at City Putt.

81

MAKE JAMBALAYA

WHAT'S THE DEAL? Jambalaya is a favorite Creole rice and sausage dish. The Mardi Gras School of Cooking *(519 Wilkinson, Suite 101, themardigrasschoolofcooking.com)* offers hands-on classes where you can discover Louisiana's fun, food, and folklore and make popular local specialties like gumbo and jambalaya.

DO IT IF: Tonight you're gonna see your cher ami-o.

SKIP IT IF: Goodby Joe, you gotta go, me oh my oh.

LOCAL ADVICE: The hands-on class at 10 am has a Bloody Mary bar.

I DID IT: ☐ #nolabucket #jambalaya

DID YOU KNOW?

Many historians believe Spanish immigrants in New Orleans created jambalaya while attempting to recreate their beloved paella with local ingredients.

82

PUMP UP THE JAM

WHAT'S THE DEAL? JAMNOLA *(2832 Royal St., jamnola.com)* is on a mission to help combat negativity through the joy of art and music. They have created an Instagrammer's heaven with 12 immersive and interactive New Orleans-themed art exhibits, unlike anything you have seen. Join a parade, meet musical icons like Satchmo, and even end up in a crawfish pot.

DO IT IF: You're on Instagram

SKIP IT IF: It's not your jam.

LOCAL ADVICE: Go on a weekday to avoid crowds or book a private tour if you really dislike strangers.

I DID IT: ☐ #nolabucket #jamnola

DID YOU KNOW?

JAMNOLA stands for "Joy, Art, Music, New Orleans, Louisiana." They believe that happiness can overcome all if you immerse yourself in it and share it with others.

83

HANG WITH VAMPIRES

WHAT'S THE DEAL? New Orleans is home to a community of modern-day Draculas. Take a vampire tour to learn their history in the French Quarter *(jonathanweisstours.com)*. Shop for vampire couture at Boutique du Vampyre *(709 St Ann St., feelthebite.com)*. Stop in for a "bite" at the Vampire Cafe *(801 Royal St. nolavampirecafe.com)*Discover dark bars like Santos *(1135 Decatur St., santosbar.com)*, where these creatures of the night gather, occasionally granting entry to mortals.

DO IT IF: You want an interview with the vampire.

SKIP IT IF: Vampires make you batty.

LOCAL ADVICE: The Boutique du Vampyre may share the secret password to the private vampire club *Potions* if you ask politely.

I DID IT: ☐ #nolabucket #lovebites

DID YOU KNOW?

Anne Rice - the undisputed queen of dark vampire literature - was born and raised in New Orleans.

84

GET HOLY AT URSULINE CONVENT

WHAT'S THE DEAL? The Ursuline order of nuns came to New Orleans in the 1700s to educate and minister to young women. The Old Ursuline Convent *(1100 Chartres St., oldursulineconventmuseum.com)* was completed in 1754, making it the oldest building in the Mississippi River valley. It is a must-stop on any self-guided walking tour of the Quarter.

DO IT IF: Get thee to a nunnery.

SKIP IT IF: Nun for me, thanks.

LOCAL ADVICE: Grab breakfast around the corner at Croissants D'Or *(617 Ursulines Ave., croissantdornola.com)*.

I DID IT: ☐　#nolabucket #barnun

DID YOU KNOW?

The uptown Ursuline Academy is the oldest continually operating Catholic school and the oldest school for girls in the United States.

85

VISIT THE ALWAYS CHRISTMAS BAR

WHAT'S THE DEAL? New Orleans is famous for dive bars, and Snake and Jake's Christmas Club Lounge *(7612 Oak St., snakeandjakes.com)* is one of the diviest. They keep their kitschy-retro Christmas decorations up year-round, making it an excellent stop for yuletide cheer any day of the year.

DO IT IF: You like to find locals in the dark.

SKIP IT IF: You haven't had a tetanus shot.

LOCAL ADVICE: The later you show up, the better. Try the Possum Drop - a shot of Jäger dropped in a pint of Schlitz beer.

I DID IT: ☐ #nolabucket #xmasbar

DID YOU KNOW?

Anthony Bourdain and George Clooney drank here, but the biggest star is Peeve, the dog. You can buy him a shot of kibble. The money goes to a local animal rescue.

86

LEARN TO BEAD FROM A MARDI GRAS INDIAN

WHAT'S THE DEAL? The New Orleans Jazz & Heritage Foundation *(1205 N. Rampart St., jazzandheritage.org)* offers seasonal workshops where you can learn unique skills from true culture-bearers, including beading a patch suitable for an authentic Mardi Gras Indian suit. One popular workshop is taught by Howard Miller, Big Chief of the Creole Wild West Mardi Gras Indian tribe.

DO IT IF: You are searching for the venerable bead.

SKIP IT IF: You're feeling strung-out.

LOCAL ADVICE: Visit the Backstreet Cultural Museum *(1531 St. Philip St., backstreetmuseum.org)* first to learn about Mardi Gras Indian culture.

I DID IT: ☐ #nolabucket #beadking

DID YOU KNOW?

Mardi Gras Indian history is shrouded in mystery, but folklore dates them back to the early 1800s. The names of their "tribes" were inspired by Native Americans, as a sign of respect and appreciation for the help enslaved Africans received when fleeing captivity.

87

BIKE ESPLANADE AVENUE

WHAT'S THE DEAL? Esplanade Avenue is famed for its stately mansions and live oak canopies. Few streets in New Orleans can compete with her beauty. Rent a bike from Bicycle Michael *(622 Frenchmen St., bicyclemichaels.com)* and enjoy the four-mile ride from the Mississippi River levee up to City Park.

DO IT IF: You want handlebars to handle the bars.

SKIP IT IF: You still need training wheels.

LOCAL ADVICE: Watch for baby Night-Herons in the 2300 block during summer nesting season.

I DID IT: ☐ #nolabucket #goodtimesroll

DID YOU KNOW?

Esplanade served as a portage route for traders in the 18th and 19th centuries, linking the Mississippi River to Bayou St. John and Lake Pontchartrain.

88

PARTY LIKE A PIRATE

WHAT'S THE DEAL? As an important trading port, New Orleans and pirate lore go hand in hand. Jean Lafitte is New Orleans' most celebrated pirate. You can raise a toast to him at Lafitte's Blacksmith Shop Bar *(941 Bourbon St., lafittesblacksmithshop.com)*. It is believed to be the oldest building used as a bar in the United States and was the likely New Orleans base of Lafitte's Barataria smuggling operation.

DO IT IF: You like your yo ho ho's with a bottle of rum.

SKIP IT IF: You are a not-so-Jolly Roger.

LOCAL ADVICE: Try the Voodoo Daiquiri, aka *Purple Drank*. Seek out the back piano bar each evening. It's a local favorite.

I DID IT: ☐ #nolabucket #ratedarrgh

DID YOU KNOW?

Jean Lafitte helped keep New Orleans out of British hands by organizing his men and fighting alongside Andrew Jackson in the "Battle of New Orleans."

89

DISCOVER YAKA MEIN

WHAT'S THE DEAL? Yaka Mein is a Creole style soup prepared with beef or chicken broth poured hot over Chinese noodles and served with secret spices and a hard-boiled egg. The famous street food is nicknamed *Old Sober* for its alleged healing powers. The dish has cured many a hangover earned during late-night French Quarter drinking sessions.

DO IT IF: You want a real New Orleans hangover cure.

SKIP IT IF: You don't like slurping or burping.

LOCAL ADVICE: Find the "Ya-Ka-Mein Lady" aka Chef Linda *(neworleanssoulfood.com)*. Manchu Food Store (1413 N Claiborne St., *manchuchicken.com*) is another favorite spot for this local delicacy.

I DID IT: ☐ #nolabucket #yakamein

DID YOU KNOW?

Yaka Mein may have started with Chinese immigrants looking to please their Creole customers or perhaps with African American soldiers who fought in WWII or the Korean War. The origins are hotly debated.

90

BANG A BUCKET DRUM FOR TIPS

WHAT'S THE DEAL? Bucket drummers are some of the most entrepreneurial street musicians in New Orleans. All they need is a five-gallon bucket, a couple of sticks, and a beat in their soul. Tip a young drummer and ask if you can sit in for a spell. See if you can earn them a few dollars with your rhythm.

DO IT IF: You want more bang for your buck.

SKIP IT IF: You want more bucks for your bangs.

LOCAL ADVICE: Bourbon Street is an excellent place to find a willing bucket drummer. Ask them to sign this page of the book.

I DID IT: ☐ #nolabucket #differentdrum

DID YOU KNOW?

Drumming is engrained in New Orleans culture. Congo Square was a designated gathering place for enslaved Africans to play their drums.

91

RIDE THE CAROUSEL

WHAT'S THE DEAL? A treasured carousel is the centerpiece of the Hines Carousel Gardens Amusement Park *(7 Victory Ave., neworleanscitypark.com/in-the-park/carousel-gardens).* Fewer than 100 hand-carved carousels remain in the United States. This one was crafted by Loof & Carmel and has 53 horses, a camel, lion, and giraffe. Locals call them flying horses. Giddyup!

DO IT IF: You feel like horsing around.

SKIP IT IF: You only ride carousels that serve drinks.

LOCAL ADVICE: Go for an exterior horse with a pole, so you don't miss out on the up and down action.

I DID IT: ☐ #nolabucket #roundandround

DID YOU KNOW?

The carousel was built in 1906, but some of the 56 animals date back to 1885. This is such a popular local attraction that the animals require repainting every two years.

92

KNOW OUR COLORFUL HISTORY

WHAT'S THE DEAL? To understand New Orleans, you must learn the stories of the cultures and people who shape her. Le Musée de f.p.c. *(2336 Esplanade Ave. lemuseedefpc.com)* is an inspiring historic house museum dedicated exclusively to preserving the material culture of and telling the story of free people of color in New Orleans.

DO IT IF: You want to learn from the past.

SKIP IT IF: You are still living in the past.

LOCAL ADVICE: Take the 10-minute stroll to Dooky Chase Restaurant *(2301 Orleans Ave., dookychaserestaurants.com)* for Creole-inspired home cooking. The black-owned eatery was a meeting place for pioneers of the civil rights movement and has hosted presidents George W. Bush and Barack Obama.

I DID IT: ☐ #nolabucket #localcolor

DID YOU KNOW?

Gens de couleur libres refers to Black People who were born free or freed before the Civil War. New Orleans was home to one of the oldest and largest populations of free people of color.

93

GO NUTS FOR PRALINES

WHAT'S THE DEAL? One of New Orleans' signature foods combines sugar, milk or cream, butter, and pecan halves to create a sweet treat people go nuts for. Most French Quarter praline shops offer free samples, and many shops make them on-site so you can watch the process. Try several and decide who you think has the best.

DO IT IF: You're developing a taste for New Orleans.

SKIP IT IF: You're developing diabetes and a nut allergy.

LOCAL ADVICE: Don't miss Loretta's Authentic Pralines *(2101 N. Rampart St., lorettaspralines.com)*, a local favorite for more than 35 years.

I DID IT: ☐ #nolabucket #deeznuts

DID YOU KNOW?

It is widely believed that the early version of the praline was brought from France by the Ursuline nuns in 1727.

94

STUDY THE
ART OF BURLESQUE

WHAT'S THE DEAL? Burlesque is as much a part of the fabric of New Orleans culture as jazz music and gumbo, and the overwhelming number of Burlesque performances all around town is proof. Some of the world's most famous strip tease artists have performed here, and our Burlesque artists today are serious about preserving their unique art form. Check out their talents by catching a show while hoping they don't catch a cold! *(eventbrite.com/d/la--new-orleans/burlesque/)* You might even pick up a few moves to take home with you!

DO IT IF: You like to strip and tease.

SKIP IT IF: You tend to trip with ease.

LOCAL ADVICE: Check out the Allways Lounge *(2240 Saint Claude Ave theallwayslounge.net)* for some unique takes on this art form like peep shows and lube wrestling.

I DID IT: ☐   #nolabucket #twistandshout

DID YOU KNOW?

New Orleans burlesque performer Blaze Starr *(1932-2015)* was infamous for her affair with a Louisiana Governor. The story was made into a movie starring Paul Newman and Lolita Davidovich.

95

GET A TASTE OF LAKE PONTCHARTRAIN

WHAT'S THE DEAL? New Orleans is famous for seafood, and nothing tops feasting on fresh fish while gazing out at the water where your dinner was swimming a few hours earlier. Lake Pontchartrain has a variety of waterfront dining options.

DO IT IF: You like fresh seafood and good views

SKIP IT IF: You get queasy sitting on the water.

LOCAL ADVICE: Hit The Blue Crab Restaurant & Oyster Bar *(7900 Lakeshore Dr., thebluecrabnola.com)*. Try the shrimp and grits.

I DID IT: ☐ #nolabucket #lakeandbake

DID YOU KNOW?

Louisiana has had a thriving seafood industry since the 1800s and is second only to Alaska in annual seafood harvest volume.

96

SHAKE SHAKE SHAKE IT ON FRENCHMEN

WHAT'S THE DEAL? The Faubourg Marigny neighborhood is to locals what the French Quarter is to tourists. Frenchmen Street has been called the most consistently musical stretch of asphalt in New Orleans. The street hosts various musical genres in iconic venues like The Spotted Cat Music Club (623 Frenchmen St., *spottedcatmusicclub.com*) and The Blue Nile (532 Frenchmen St., *bluenilelive.com*).

DO IT IF: You love the local jam.

SKIP IT IF: Blueberry is your jam.

LOCAL ADVICE: Go early for small plate dining at Three Muses *(536 Frenchmen St., 3musesnola.com).* Reservations recommended.

I DID IT: ☐ #nolabucket #frenchmen

DID YOU KNOW?

Frenchmen Street got its name after several Frenchmen were killed by a brutal Spanish mercenary, General Alejandro "Bloody" O'Reilly.

97

SHOP A
MARDI GRAS STORE

WHAT'S THE DEAL? New Orleans has Mardi Gras stores solely dedicated to selling Mardi Gras themed throws and trinkets to krewes and visitors. Beads, wigs, tutus, and other Carnival novelties are available at great prices. Stop in for some merch and turn your hotel room into Mardi Gras central.

DO IT IF: You love shiny objects.

SKIP IT IF: You are tutu tired.

LOCAL ADVICE: Plush Appeal *(2812 Toulouse St., mardigrasspot.com)* is the favorite spot for local krewe captains.

I DID IT: ☐   #nolabucket #shinyhappypeople

DID YOU KNOW?

Mardi Gras colors date back to King of Rex in 1872. A later parade theme revealed their often-contested meanings, with purple representing justice, green representing faith, and gold representing power.

98

DIVE INTO
BABY DOLL CULTURE

WHAT'S THE DEAL? The Black Storyville Baby Dolls were the first all-female marching krewe. You can learn about them and other early African American cultural organizations at the small but mighty Backstreet Cultural Museum *(1531 St. Philip St., backstreetmuseum.org)*. Funerals, Second Lines, and Mardi Gras Indians are among the featured exhibits.

DO IT IF: You want to learn about culture bearers.

SKIP IT IF: You can't bear learning about culture.

LOCAL ADVICE: Grab breakfast around the corner at Lil' Dizzy's *(1500 Esplanade Ave., lildizzyscafe.net)*. Don't forget to ask for a homemade biscuit.

I DID IT: ☐ #nolabucket #babydoll

DID YOU KNOW?

The Backstreet Museum was once home to the Blandin Funeral Home.

99

SEE WHAT'S
IN YOUR CARDS

WHAT'S THE DEAL? New Orleans is home to countless spiritual practitioners, and card reading is one of the most prolific divination forms in the city. Jackson Square serves as a home base for many of our mystics throwing tarot. Sit for a reading to see what's in your cards.

DO IT IF: The future's so bright you have to wear shades.

SKIP IT IF: You're here with the Westboro Baptist Church

LOCAL ADVICE: Go early in the day on the weekend for the best selection and availability of readers. Walk around and make eye contact until you feel a connection.

I DID IT: ☐ #nolabucket #cardashians

DID YOU KNOW?

Many of the tarot cards' images were inspired by the Venice Carnival parades' costumed figures.

100

DINE ON A PADDLEWHEELER

WHAT'S THE DEAL? Paddlewheeler riverboats have been rolling on the Mississippi River since the 1800s. Dine on the *Creole Queen (creolequeen.com)* or *Natchez (steamboatnachez.com)* for an unforgettable New Orleans experience right out of a Mark Twain story.

DO IT IF: Paddlewheelers float your boat.

SKIP IT IF: You get seasick.

LOCAL ADVICE: Take a dinner cruise for stunning city views as you return to the dock.

I DID IT: ☐ #nolabucket #bigwheel

DID YOU KNOW?

Before the steamship was invented, travel on the Mississippi River around New Orleans was dominated by shallow draft, pole-powered riverboats.

101

TRAVERSE TULANE

WHAT'S THE DEAL? Tulane University *(6823 St. Charles Ave., tulane.edu)* is a private research university founded in 1834. Their 110-acre campus boasts impressive architecture and stately live oaks. It is a favorite stroll for New Orleans residents.

DO IT IF: You want to get schooled.

SKIP IT IF: You are too cool for school.

LOCAL ADVICE: Read up on the Banana King and check out his house *(near 6915 St. Charles Ave).* **Crêpes** à **la Cart** *(1039 Broadway St., crepesalacartnola.com)* is a student street food favorite.

I DID IT: ☐ #nolabucket #seconddegree

DID YOU KNOW?

Tulane University alumni include twelve Louisiana governors, Congress members, 18 Rhodes Scholars, and two Nobel Prize Laureates.

102

GET THRIFTY-STYLEY

WHAT'S THE DEAL? Dress like a local by adopting the New Orleans thrift store style. Some of the best thrift shops and vintage clothing stores are on Magazine Street. To start, check Buffalo Exchange *(4119 Magazine St., buffaloexchange.com)* and the Funky Monkey *(3127 Magazine St., funkymonkeynola.com).*

DO IT IF: You wear my grandpa's clothes. You look incredible.

SKIP IT IF: You're gonna pop some tags.

LOCAL ADVICE: Go early in the day and start off with a donut at District Donuts *(2209 Magazine St., districtdonuts.com)*

I DID IT: ☐ #nolabucket #thrifty

DID YOU KNOW?

Wearing vintage makes you your own kind of beautiful.

103

EAT A
VIETNAMESE PO-BOY

WHAT'S THE DEAL? New Orleans and Vietnam have similar climates, predominately Catholic populations, and they were both French colonies at one time. This led to cultural exchanges that landed on New Orleans plates with intriguing blends of Cajun and Vietnamese foods. Try a Banh-mi. It's a Vietnamese Po-Boy.

DO IT IF: You like learning about other cultures through food.

SKIP IT IF: You are afraid to try anything new.

LOCAL ADVICE: Try the spicy pork Banh-mi at local favorite Lilly's Café *(1813 Magazine Street, facebook.com/LillysCafe)* in the Lower Garden District, and stroll Magazine when you're finished with lunch.

I DID IT: ☐   #nolabucket #banhmi

DID YOU KNOW?

In the mid-70s, many Vietnamese people settled in New Orleans after fleeing their home country to escape the incoming Communist regime. Over 14,000 Vietnamese live in the greater New Orleans metro area.

104

DOWNWARD DOG ON THE RIVERBANK

WHAT'S THE DEAL? Everything is better on the banks of the Mississippi, including yoga. The continually flowing water creates a perfectly Zen environment. If you have your own routine, grab your mat, take a deep breath, head to the river, and find your groove. You won't get any bad looks for catching a flow here.

DO IT IF: You want to feel like Benji and Adriene.

SKIP IT IF: You have a different dog position in mind on this trip.

LOCAL ADVICE: Reward yourself with some beignets to go from Café du Monde *(800 Decatur St.)* when you're finished.

I DID IT: ☐ #nolabucket #nolamaste

DID YOU KNOW?

Yoga is a group of spiritual development practices designed to train the body and mind and cultivate awareness, self-regulation, and higher consciousness. Yoga originated in Ancient India as early as 3000 BCE.

105

TRY ON BIG HATS

WHAT'S THE DEAL? Nothing makes you feel fancy like a brand new ornately decorated hat. Fleur de Paris *(523 Royal St., fdphats.com)* is the largest millinery in North America. It has the best selection on this side of gay Paris.

DO IT IF: You want to be brimming with excitement.

SKIP IT IF: You have head lice.

LOCAL ADVICE: Enjoy a frozen Irish coffee around the corner at Molly's Irish Pub *(732 Toulouse St.)*, wearing your new chapeau.

I DID IT: ☐ #nolabucket #madhatter

DID YOU KNOW?

Popular New Orleans head accessories include headbands, fascinators, top hats, fedoras, cloches, bonnets, and pillbox hats.

106

JAZZ IT UP

WHAT'S THE DEAL? It is widely believed that Jazz music was born in New Orleans. The New Orleans Jazz Museum *(400 Esplanade Ave., nolajazzmuseum.org)* hosts live performances, events, and houses more than 25,000 jazz-related artifacts.

DO IT IF: You love music and learning its history.

SKIP IT IF: You think Lawrence Welk is a hep cat.

LOCAL ADVICE: Go on a Tuesday for one of the museum's free outdoor concerts.

I DID IT: ☐   #nolabucket #wheresthefreshprince

DID YOU KNOW?

The Jazz Museum is housed in the former New Orleans U.S. Mint Building. The mint produced currency with a total value of more than $307 million, mostly in gold and silver coins.

107

STROLL
LONGUE VUE GARDENS

WHAT'S THE DEAL? Longue Vue House & Gardens (7 Bamboo Rd., *longuevue.com*) is a historic home turned museum that helped shape 20th Century society, politics, and art in New Orleans. A fantastic oasis in the middle of the city, the grounds are ideal for strolling and relaxing.

DO IT IF: You're longing to view a garden.

SKIP IT IF: You are terrified of butterflies and goldfish.

LOCAL ADVICE: Go on a day when Longue Vue has a lunch concert and pack a picnic.

I DID IT: ☐ #nolabucket #nicevue

DID YOU KNOW?

Edgar and Edith Stern married in 1921 and envisioned a peaceful place of elegance in the heart of New Orleans. They began developing the Longue Vue property the same year.

108

GET WIGGY WITH IT

WHAT'S THE DEAL? Fifi Mahony's *(934 Royal St., facebook.com/fifimahonys)* is a wig salon favored by Mardi Gras krewes for their elaborate selection of decorated wigs in fantasy colors. Their friendly staff will help you find your new alter ego.

DO IT IF: You want to see what the witness protection program feels like.

SKIP IT IF: You're looking for the hair of the dog.

LOCAL ADVICE: Go early for undivided attention. Buy a wig cap for $5.00 and try on all the wigs you wish.

I DID IT: ☐ #nolabucket #gettinwiggywithit

DID YOU KNOW?

Wigs were first documented in Ancient Egypt around 2700 BCE. They served as a status symbol and kept the head free from unwanted pests.

109

STALK THE RICH AND FAMOUS

WHAT'S THE DEAL? The Garden District's elegant mansions have been sought after by celebrities and millionaires since they began building them in the 1800s. Learn about the lifestyles of the rich and famous on a walking tour with Lucky Bean Tours *(luckybeantours.com)* or Two Chicks Walking Tours *(twochickswalkingtours.com)*. Both specialize in this area.

DO IT IF: You like elegant mansions.

SKIP IT IF: You're like Charles Manson.

LOCAL ADVICE: Go on a weekday and book a morning tour as they are generally less crowded, and cooler in the summertime.

I DID IT: ☐ #nolabucket #stalkeralert

DID YOU KNOW?

Anne Rice, John Goodman, Sandra Bullock, and Archie Manning are a few celebrities who live or have lived in the Garden District. Brad Pitt, Nicholas Cage, Emeril Lagasse, Lil Wayne, and Drew Brees own homes in New Orleans.

110

SAY FAREWELL
WITH A TOAST

WHAT'S THE DEAL?
We never say "goodbye" to New Orleans, only "Farewell, for now." It has become tradition for visitors to toast the Crescent City on their way out of town. No matter if you chose a Sazerac, Pimms Cup, Café au Lait with chicory, or a Lavender Lemonade, raise a glass to our fair city, toast to your return in the future, and let the drink warm your soul like the people of New Orleans have.

DO IT IF: You want to return to New Orleans.

SKIP IT IF: You were mugged on Bourbon Street and are never coming back.

LOCAL ADVICE: Go ahead and pick your own watering hole. If you've made it this far, you're pretty much a local now.

I DID IT: ☐ #nolabucket #illbeback

DID YOU KNOW?

One old adage that has been proven time and time again here in the Crescent City—if you love New Orleans, she will love you back.

ABOUT THE AUTHORS

Loretta-Maria Adkins is a New Orleans author with a resume that includes cab driver, camp counselor, exotic dancer, radio personality, bartender, innkeeper, travel agent, and tour guide. She is the founder of Clean Getaway Travel and a member of the New Orleans Pussyfooters.

theneworleansbucketlist@gmail.com

David L. Sloan is an author, publisher, and founder of the *100 Offbeat Adventures* Bucket List series. He started visiting New Orleans in 1986.

david@phantompress.com

Hey partner, don't be shy
Come on down here and give us a try
You wanna do some livin' before you die
Do it down in New Orleans.

Randy Newman
Down In New Orleans
The Princess and the Frog
Performed by Dr. John

Made in the USA
Middletown, DE
07 November 2023

42113735R00070